Crypto 101

The Essential Guide to Understanding and Investing in Cryptocurrencies

Content

PREFACE

Crypto 101: The Essential Guide to Understanding and Investing in Cryptocurrencies

Cryptocurrencies have taken the world by storm in the past few years, revolutionizing the way we think about money, finance, and investment. Despite the hype and excitement surrounding cryptocurrencies, many people are still unsure of what they are, how they work, and how to invest in them. This book is designed to be a beginner's guide to the world of cryptocurrency, providing an overview of the technology, the various types of cryptocurrencies, and the potential investment opportunities. It aims to demystify the world of cryptocurrency and provide a clear, concise, and accessible introduction to this exciting and rapidly evolving field. Whether you're a complete newcomer to the world of finance or a seasoned investor looking to diversify your portfolio, this book will provide you with the information you need to make informed decisions about investing in cryptocurrencies. It covers everything from the basics of blockchain technology to the most popular cryptocurrencies, such as Bitcoin, Ethereum, and Litecoin.

The book is divided into three parts:

Part 1 provides an introduction to cryptocurrency and blockchain technology, covering the history and evolution of digital currencies, the basics of blockchain technology, and the potential applications of cryptocurrencies in various industries.

Part 2 delves into the most popular cryptocurrencies, providing an overview of their features, strengths, and weaknesses. It also explores the different ways to invest in cryptocurrencies, including buying and holding, trading, and mining.

Part 3 covers some of the challenges and risks associated with investing in cryptocurrencies, as well as strategies for managing these risks. It also provides some practical advice for beginners, such as how to choose a cryptocurrency exchange, how to store and secure your cryptocurrencies, and how to avoid common mistakes.

We hope that this book will provide you with a solid foundation for understanding and investing in cryptocurrencies. We also hope that it will inspire you to explore this exciting and rapidly evolving field further, and to become a part of the growing community of cryptocurrency enthusiasts and investors.

INTRODUCTION

Cryptocurrency is a form of digital currency that uses encryption techniques to regulate the generation of new units and verify the transfer of funds. Cryptocurrencies operate independently of central banks and are not backed by any physical commodity. Instead, their value is based on a consensus among users that the currency has value and can be used as a medium of exchange.

The history of cryptocurrency can be traced back to the late 1990s, when researchers attempted to create a decentralized digital currency. However, it wasn't until the release of Bitcoin in 2009 that cryptocurrency gained widespread attention. Bitcoin was created by an unknown individual or group using the pseudonym Satoshi Nakamoto, and it quickly gained popularity due to its decentralized nature and the ability to transfer funds anonymously.

One of the main benefits of cryptocurrency is that it allows for secure, fast, and low-cost transactions. Because cryptocurrencies are decentralized and use blockchain technology, there is no need for intermediaries like banks or payment processors. This means that transactions can be completed quickly and at a lower cost than traditional payment methods.

Another benefit of cryptocurrency is that it can be used as a hedge against inflation and government intervention. Since cryptocurrencies are not tied to a government or central bank, their value is not affected by changes in government policy or inflation. This makes them a popular choice for investors who want to diversify their portfolios.

However, there are also some potential drawbacks to using cryptocurrency. For one, the value of cryptocurrencies can be highly volatile, making them a risky investment. Additionally, cryptocurrencies can be vulnerable to hacking and other security breaches, which can result in significant losses for users.

Despite these potential drawbacks, the popularity of cryptocurrency continues to grow. Today, there are thousands of different cryptocurrencies in the market, each with its own unique features and value proposition. Some of the most popular cryptocurrencies besides Bitcoin include Ethereum, Litecoin, and Ripple.

As cryptocurrency continues to evolve, it is important for individuals and businesses to stay informed about the latest trends and developments. Whether you are interested in investing in cryptocurrency, using it as a payment method, or simply learning more about this exciting new technology, there are many resources available to help you get started. An example is **Crypto 102: Beyond the Basics of Crypto.**

CHAPTER ONE

INTRODUCTION TO CRYPTOCURRENCY

Cryptocurrency is a digital or virtual currency that uses cryptography (a complex method of secure communication) to ensure secure transactions and to control the creation of new units. It operates independently of a central bank and can be transferred directly between individuals without the need for intermediaries like banks.

Cryptocurrencies operate on a decentralized network, which means that they are not controlled by any central authority. Instead, they are managed by a network of computers that collectively verify and process transactions. This process is known as mining, and it involves solving complex mathematical equations in order to validate transactions and add them to the blockchain.

The blockchain is a digital ledger that records every transaction that occurs on the network. Each block on the blockchain contains a record of several transactions, and once a block is added to the chain, it cannot be altered or deleted. This makes the blockchain an immutable record of all transactions that have occurred on the network.

When a user wants to send cryptocurrency to another user, they broadcast a transaction to the network. This transaction includes the amount of cryptocurrency being sent, the recipient's address, and a digital signature that verifies the transaction. The transaction is then broadcast to all nodes on the network, which validate and process the transaction.

To validate a transaction, nodes on the network must solve a complex mathematical equation. This equation involves using the transaction data to create a unique digital signature, which is then verified by other nodes on the network. Once the equation is solved and the transaction is verified, it is added to the blockchain.

Mining is the process by which new units of cryptocurrency are generated. Miners are individuals or groups of individuals who use powerful computers to solve complex mathematical equations in order to validate transactions and add them to the blockchain. In exchange for their work, miners are rewarded with a certain number of newly generated units of cryptocurrency.

The amount of cryptocurrency that is generated through mining is controlled by the network's algorithm. This algorithm is designed to ensure that the rate of new units being generated is consistent over time. In the case of Bitcoin, for example, the rate of new units being generated is halved every four years, with the total number of units eventually capping at 21 million.

In addition to mining, users can also acquire cryptocurrency through purchasing it on an exchange or receiving it as payment for goods or services. Once a user has acquired cryptocurrency, they can store it in a digital wallet. A digital wallet is a software program that allows users to store, send, and receive cryptocurrency.

Cryptocurrency transactions are secured through the use of encryption techniques. Each transaction is encrypted using a public key and a private key. The public key is a string of characters that serves as the user's address on the network. The private key is a separate string of characters that is used to sign transactions and prove ownership of the cryptocurrency.

When a user sends cryptocurrency to another user, they broadcast the transaction to the network along with their public key. The recipient then uses the sender's public key to decrypt the transaction and verify its validity. Once the transaction is verified, the recipient's digital wallet is updated with the new balance.

Overall, the process of how cryptocurrencies work is complex and involves multiple steps, including mining, validation, and encryption. However, the decentralized nature of the network allows for secure and fast transactions without the need for intermediaries like banks or other financial institutions. As cryptocurrency continues to evolve and gain widespread adoption, it is important for individuals and businesses to understand how it works and how it can be used as a medium of exchange.

History of cryptocurrency

Cryptocurrency, a digital or virtual currency that uses cryptography to secure and verify transactions and to control the creation of new units, has a relatively short history that dates back to the late 20th century.

The concept of a digital currency was first introduced in the 1980s, when computer scientist David Chaum proposed a cryptographic digital currency called "ecash". This currency aimed to provide anonymity and privacy to its users by encrypting transactions and using a third-party auditor to prevent fraud.

In 2008, the pseudonymous person or group of people known as Satoshi Nakamoto published a whitepaper titled "Bitcoin: A Peer-to-Peer Electronic Cash System". The paper introduced the concept of a decentralized digital currency that used a public ledger called the blockchain to record transactions and prevent double-spending. Bitcoin's decentralized nature allowed it to operate without the need for a central authority or intermediary, such as a bank.

Bitcoin was launched in 2009, and the first transaction took place between Satoshi Nakamoto and a programmer named Hal Finney. Over the next few years, Bitcoin gained popularity among early adopters in the tech community and began to gain wider recognition.

In 2011, other cryptocurrencies, such as Litecoin and Namecoin, were launched, and the concept of cryptocurrency gained even more attention. The growth of cryptocurrency led to the creation of numerous exchanges and wallets to facilitate the buying, selling, and storage of cryptocurrencies.

In 2013, the value of Bitcoin reached an all-time high of over $1,000, and other cryptocurrencies also saw significant growth. However, this period was also marked by several high-profile incidents, such as the collapse of the Mt. Gox exchange, which lost hundreds of thousands of Bitcoins, and the shutdown of the Silk Road, an online black market that used Bitcoin for transactions.

Despite these setbacks, cryptocurrency continued to gain acceptance and recognition. In 2014, Microsoft began accepting Bitcoin payments for Xbox and Windows digital content, and the following year, the New York State Department of Financial Services introduced BitLicense, a regulatory framework for businesses operating with virtual currencies.

The growth of cryptocurrency continued throughout the 2010s, with the introduction of new cryptocurrencies such as Ethereum, Ripple, and Bitcoin Cash, and the rise of initial coin offerings (ICOs), a method of crowd funding that uses cryptocurrency instead of traditional funding methods.

In 2017, Bitcoin saw a massive surge in value, reaching an all-time high of nearly $20,000. This growth led to increased mainstream attention and interest in cryptocurrency, as well as increased regulation and scrutiny.

Today, cryptocurrency continues to be a rapidly evolving and controversial field, with advocates touting its potential to disrupt traditional financial systems and detractors warning of the risks of unregulated digital currencies.

Benefits of cryptocurrency

The benefits of cryptocurrency will be compared to other conventional currencies both for domestic and international transactions.

1. Decentralization: One of the primary benefits of cryptocurrency is that it is decentralized, meaning that

it operates without a central authority or intermediary like a bank. This allows for greater transparency, security, and privacy, and removes the need for traditional financial institutions to facilitate transactions.

2. Security: Cryptocurrency transactions are secured by complex cryptography and blockchain technology, making them difficult to hack or counterfeit. This reduces the risk of fraud and provides greater security for users.

3. Lower transaction fees: Since cryptocurrencies operate without intermediaries, transaction fees are typically much lower than those charged by traditional financial institutions, making them an attractive option for people who want to avoid high fees.

4. Fast and efficient transactions: Cryptocurrency transactions are processed quickly and efficiently, as they are conducted directly between two parties without the need for intermediaries or lengthy verification processes.

5. Privacy: Cryptocurrency transactions are usually anonymous and can provide greater privacy and security than traditional financial transactions, which can be tracked and monitored by government agencies or other third parties.

6. Global access: Cryptocurrency can be used by anyone with an internet connection, regardless of their location or economic status. This allows for greater financial inclusion and access to financial services for people who may not have access to traditional banking systems.

7. Potential for investment: Cryptocurrency has the potential to appreciate in value over time, making it an attractive investment option for people looking to diversify their portfolios.

It's important to remember that while there are potential benefits to cryptocurrency, there are also risks and uncertainties associated with this fast evolving technology. It's pertinent to do your own research and understand the risks before investing in or using cryptocurrency. As we progress, we will see some of the risks and how to curb and avoid the avoidable.

CHAPTER TWO

BLOCKCHAIN TECHNOLOGY

Blockchain technology is a decentralized and distributed digital ledger that is used to record transactions in a secure and transparent way. It uses cryptography to secure the information and is maintained by a network of computers rather than a central authority. Each block in the chain contains a record of several transactions and is linked to the previous block, creating a chain of blocks (hence the name "blockchain"). Once a block is added to the chain, it cannot be altered, making the system highly secure and resistant to tampering. Blockchain technology is used to power cryptocurrencies like Bitcoin, but it has many other potential applications in areas like supply chain management, voting systems, and more.

In a simpler language; Imagine you have a notebook in which you keep a record of all the money you have spent and received. Now imagine that instead of one notebook, there are thousands of copies of the notebook, each owned by different people, and each person can add a record of a transaction to their own notebook. This is what the blockchain is: a digital ledger that records transactions, but instead of one copy, there are many copies of the ledger, all owned by different people.

Each time a transaction is added to the blockchain, it is verified by a network of computers, and once it is verified, it is added to a block. Each block contains a record of several transactions, and once a block is added to the blockchain, it cannot be altered or deleted. This makes the blockchain very secure and resistant to tampering, since if someone tries to alter a block, all the other copies of the blockchain will see that the block is different and reject it.

Because the blockchain is a distributed ledger, there is no central authority that controls it. Instead, it is maintained by a network of computers that work together to verify transactions and add them to the blockchain. This makes the blockchain very transparent, since everyone in the network can see the transactions that have been recorded.

Types of Blockchains

There are three main types of blockchains:

Public, private, and hybrid

1. Public blockchains: Public blockchains are decentralized and open to anyone who wants to participate in the network. This means that anyone can read the blockchain's contents and write transactions to it. Public blockchains are secured through a consensus mechanism, such as proof-of-work or proof-of-stake, which allows the network to agree on the state of the blockchain without the need for a central authority.

Because public blockchains are open to everyone, they are highly transparent and anyone can view the transactions that have been recorded on the blockchain. This also means that public blockchains are highly resistant to censorship and are not controlled by any single entity. Bitcoin and Ethereum are two of the most well-known public blockchains.

2. Private Blockchains: Private Blockchains are operated by a single organization or group of organizations with specific permissions to access and write to the blockchain. They are not open to the public, and transactions are only visible to members of the network. Private Blockchains are often used for internal business processes, supply chain management, or other industry-specific use cases.

Because private blockchains are not open to the public, they can be designed with specific privacy and security features that are tailored to the needs of the organization using the blockchain. Private Blockchains can also be faster and more efficient than public blockchains, since they don't have to deal with as many nodes on the network. However, private blockchains are more centralized and can be more vulnerable to attacks or corruption.

3. Hybrid blockchains: Hybrid blockchains are a combination of public and private blockchains. They allow for public access to certain parts of the blockchain, while other parts are restricted to members of a specific group or organization. Hybrid blockchains are useful for cases where some data needs to be kept private, while other data needs to be shared publicly.

For example, a company might use a hybrid blockchain to share certain supply chain information with the public, while keeping other sensitive information private. Hybrid blockchains can also allow for interoperability between different blockchain networks, which can be useful for businesses that need to share information with partners on different blockchain networks. Overall, the type of blockchain that is used depends on the specific use case and the needs of the organization using the blockchain. Each type of blockchain has its own advantages and disadvantages, and it's important to choose the right type of blockchain for the job at hand.

Advantages and Disadvantages

Here are some advantages and disadvantages of each type of blockchain.

Advantages of Public Blockchain

- High transparency: anyone can view transactions on the blockchain, making it difficult to manipulate or censor.
- Decentralized: public blockchains are not controlled by any single entity, making them resistant to censorship and corruption.
- Security: public blockchains are secured through consensus mechanisms, making it very difficult to hack or attack the network.

Disadvantages of Public Blockchain

- Scalability: as more users join the network, public blockchains can become slower and less efficient.
- Privacy: because public blockchains are transparent, transactions are visible to everyone, which can be a

disadvantage for individuals or organizations that need to keep their transactions private.

- Energy consumption: some public blockchains, such as Bitcoin, require a lot of energy to operate, which can be a concern for environmental reasons.

Advantages of Private Blockchain

- Privacy: private blockchains can be designed with specific privacy features that are tailored to the needs of the organization using the Blockchain.
- Speed: because private blockchains don't have to deal with as many nodes on the network, they can be faster and more efficient than public blockchains.
- Control: private blockchains are operated by a single entity, which gives that entity more control over the network.

Disadvantages of Private Blockchain

- Centralized: private blockchains are controlled by a single entity, which makes them more vulnerable to attacks or corruption.
- Less transparent: because private blockchains are not open to the public, they can be less transparent than public blockchains.

- Interoperability: private blockchains can be more difficult to integrate with other blockchains or systems.

Advantages of Hybrid Blockchain

- Flexibility: hybrid blockchains allow for public access to certain parts of the blockchain, while keeping other parts private, which can be useful for organizations that need to share some information publicly, but keep other information private.
- Interoperability: hybrid blockchains can allow for interoperability between different blockchain networks, which can be useful for businesses that need to share information with partners on different blockchain networks.
- Security: like public blockchains, hybrid blockchains are secured through consensus mechanisms, making it very difficult to hack or attack the network.

Disadvantages of Hybrid Blockchain

- Complexity: hybrid blockchains can be more complex to design and operate than public or private blockchains.

- Governance: hybrid blockchains require careful governance to ensure that public and private parts of the network are properly balanced and secure.
- Limited scalability: like public blockchains, hybrid blockchains can become slower and less efficient as more users join the network.

Sit tight as we look into the first coin and understand it technicalities alongside other coins.

CHAPTER THREE

BITCOIN AND ALTCOINS

What is Bitcoin?

Bitcoin is a digital currency, also known as a cryptocurrency, which was created in 2009 by an unknown person or group of people using the pseudonym Satoshi Nakamoto. Bitcoin operates on a decentralized network, meaning that it is not controlled by any government or financial institution. Instead, it uses blockchain technology to record transactions and ensure the security of the network.

One of the key features of Bitcoin is that it allows for peer-to-peer transactions without the need for intermediaries like banks. Transactions are recorded on the blockchain, a public ledger that is maintained by a network of computers around the world. Bitcoin transactions are validated by network participants called miners, who use their computing power to solve complex mathematical equations and earn newly minted bitcoins as a reward.

Bitcoin is known for its scarcity, as there is a limit of 21 million bitcoins that can ever be created. This limit is built into the protocol, and the rate at which new bitcoins are created decreases over time. Bitcoin is also highly volatile, with its value fluctuating rapidly in response to market demand.

While Bitcoin was initially used primarily as a means of payment, it has also become an attractive investment vehicle due to its potential for high returns.

Buying and Storing Bitcoins

To buy and store Bitcoin, you will need to follow these general steps:

1. Choose a reputable Bitcoin exchange: There are many cryptocurrency exchanges available, but not all are trustworthy. Choose a reputable exchange that is regulated and has a good track record of security.

2. Create an account: Follow the exchange's instructions to create an account. This will typically involve providing some personal information, such as your name, address, and email.

3. Verify your identity: To comply with anti-money laundering (AML) and know-your-customer (KYC) regulations, you may need to provide additional

documentation to verify your identity, such as a passport or driver's license.

4. Fund your account: To buy Bitcoin, you will need to fund your account with fiat currency, such as US dollars or euros. You can typically do this by bank transfer, credit card, or other payment methods supported by the exchange.

5. Buy Bitcoin: Once your account is funded, you can buy Bitcoin using the exchange's trading platform. The process will vary depending on the exchange, but typically involves specifying the amount of Bitcoin you want to buy and the price you are willing to pay.

6. Store your Bitcoin: Once you have bought Bitcoin, you will need to store it in a digital wallet. There are many different types of wallets available, including software wallets, hardware wallets, and paper wallets. Choose a wallet that suits your needs and follow the instructions to set it up.

7. Keep your Bitcoin secure: Bitcoin is a valuable asset, and you should take steps to keep it secure. This includes using a strong password, enabling two-factor authentication, and keeping your private keys safe. If you store your Bitcoin on a hardware wallet, keep it in a safe place and make sure to back up your seed phrase.

How to choose a wallet will be discussed in chapter six. Since they are many caricature wallet out there to steal both funds and identity, one need to be careful.

Bitcoin along with other cryptocurrency can be bought in bits. This means that you do not have to buy a whole bitcoin. You can start with a fraction. Most exchangers allows a minimum of ten US Dollars ($10) worth of bitcoin or any cryptocurrency while some others allows fifty US Dollars ($50) as minimum.

What is Altcoin?

Altcoin is short for "alternative coin," which refers to any cryptocurrency that is not Bitcoin. While Bitcoin was the first and most well-known cryptocurrency, there are now thousands of altcoins in circulation, each with their own unique features and characteristics.

Like Bitcoin, altcoins are typically based on blockchain technology, which allows for secure and decentralized transactions without the need for a central authority. However, each altcoin may have its own specific use case, such as faster transaction times, improved privacy, or more efficient mining algorithms.

Some examples of popular altcoins include Ethereum, Litecoin, Ripple, and Bitcoin Cash. Each of these coins has its own unique features and benefits, which can make them attractive to investors and users alike.

Investing in altcoins can be a high-risk, high-reward proposition, as the value of these coins can be highly volatile. It's important to do your own research and understand the risks before investing in any altcoin. Additionally, it's important to store your altcoins securely in a digital wallet, and to be aware of potential scams and fraudulent projects in the cryptocurrency space.

Types of altcoins

We already know that altcoins is any coin other than bitcoin and so you will be correct to mention any coin here. However we will categorize them based on purpose and feature.

1. Ethereum and Smart Contract Coins: Ethereum is a blockchain platform that allows developers to build decentralized applications (DApps) using smart contracts. Many altcoins have been built on top of the Ethereum blockchain, and they are often referred to as

"ERC-20" tokens. Other smart contract coins include Cardano, EOS, and NEO.

2. Privacy Coins: Privacy coins are cryptocurrencies designed to provide users with enhanced anonymity and privacy. Examples of privacy coins include Monero, Zcash, and Dash.

3. Stablecoins: Stablecoins are cryptocurrencies that are designed to maintain a stable value by being pegged to a real-world asset like a fiat currency or a commodity. Examples of stablecoins include Tether, USD Coin, and Dai.

4. Gaming Coins: Gaming coins are cryptocurrencies that are designed for use within online games and gaming platforms. Examples of gaming coins include Enjin Coin, Decentraland, and FunFair.

5. Utility Tokens: Utility tokens are cryptocurrencies that are designed to be used within a specific ecosystem or platform. They are often used as a means of payment or reward within the platform. Examples of utility tokens include Basic Attention Token (BAT), Chainlink (LINK), and Binance Coin (BNB).

6. Proof-of-Stake Coins: Proof-of-stake (PoS) is an alternative consensus mechanism to Bitcoin's proof-of-work (PoW) consensus. PoS coins allow users to validate transactions and earn rewards by holding coins and

staking them on the network. Examples of PoS coins include Cardano, Polkadot, and Tezos.

7. Decentralized Finance Coins: Decentralized finance (DeFi) refers to financial applications built on blockchain technology that allow users to access financial services without the need for traditional intermediaries. DeFi coins include Aave, Uniswap, and Compound.

8. Hybrid coins: These are altcoins that combine elements of multiple types of coins, or have unique features that don't fit neatly into any one category. Examples include Bitcoin Cash (BCH), which aims to improve on Bitcoin's scalability and transaction speed, and Dogecoin (DOGE), which started as a meme but has gained popularity as a payment method and social media tipping tool.

9. Directed Acyclic Graph (DAG) coins: These are altcoins that use a DAG structure rather than a traditional blockchain, allowing for faster transaction processing and scalability. Examples include IOTA (MIOTA), Nano (NANO), and Byteball (GBYTE).

10. Smart contract platform coins: These are altcoins that provide a platform for developers to create and execute smart contracts, which are self-executing contracts with the terms of the agreement written into code. Examples include Ethereum (ETH), EOS (EOS), and TRON (TRX).

Buying and Storing Altcoins.

There is no much difference with buying and storing altcoins with buying and storing bitcoin. The difference may be that some wallets are dedicated for a specific altcoin. Using a general wallet will do the trick.

Here is a brief step to buy and store altcoin.

Buying Altcoin

1. Choose a cryptocurrency exchange: There are many cryptocurrency exchanges where you can buy altcoins, such as Binance, Coinbase, Kraken, and Gemini. Research the exchange and make sure it supports the altcoin you want to purchase.

2. Set up an account: Sign up for an account on the exchange and complete the required verification process.

3. Add funds: Add funds to your account using a bank transfer, credit card, or other payment methods supported by the exchange.

4. Buy altcoins: Once your funds have been added to your account, you can use them to buy the altcoin you want. Make sure to select the correct altcoin and enter the amount you want to purchase.

Storing Altcoin

1. Choose a wallet: There are several types of wallets you can use to store your altcoins, including hardware wallets, software wallets, and mobile wallets. Research the different types of wallets and choose one that suits your needs.
2. Set up a wallet: Follow the instructions provided by the wallet provider to set up your wallet. Make sure to write down your seed phrase and store it in a safe place.
3. Transfer your altcoins: Once your wallet is set up, transfer your altcoins from the exchange to your wallet. Make sure to double-check the wallet address to avoid any errors.
4. Keep your wallet secure: Keep your seed phrase and private keys in a safe place, and avoid sharing them with anyone. Use two-factor authentication to enhance the security of your wallet.

Things to consider when buying and storing altcoins

Here are some things to consider when buying and storing altcoins:

1. Research the Altcoin: Before buying any altcoin, it's important to do your research and understand its underlying technology, use cases, and potential risks. Look for information on the altcoin's whitepaper, team, community, and market performance.

2. Choose a Reputable Exchange: Select a reputable cryptocurrency exchange with a track record of security and reliability. Research the exchange's reputation, history, and security measures.

3. Secure Your Account: Use strong passwords, two-factor authentication (2FA), and other security measures to protect your exchange account.

4. Diversify Your Portfolio: Consider diversifying your altcoin portfolio by investing in multiple altcoins from different categories, such as privacy coins, gaming coins, and stablecoins. This can help reduce your risk and increase potential returns.

5. Select a Secure Wallet: Choose a secure wallet to store your altcoins. Hardware wallets are generally considered to be the most secure, but software wallets and mobile wallets can also be safe if used properly.

6. Keep Your Private Keys Safe: Your private keys are the only way to access your altcoins, so it's crucial to keep them safe. Store your private keys offline and avoid sharing them with anyone.

7. Keep Your Seed Phrase Safe: Your seed phrase is a set of words that can be used to recover your wallet in case of loss or damage. Keep your seed phrase offline and store it in a secure location.

8. Monitor Your Investments: Keep track of your altcoin investments and monitor market trends and news. This can help you make informed decisions and adjust your portfolio accordingly.

Note that no two altcoin has the same name and blockchain support. So Bitcoin on ERC20 is completely different from BitcoinX in ERC20. And Tron on TRC20 is different from Tron on ADL40. The latter is most likely a caricature of the original aimed at stealing fund.

CHAPTER FOUR

MINING

Crypto mining is the process of verifying transactions on a blockchain network and adding them to the blockchain ledger in exchange for newly created cryptocurrency tokens. In other words, miners use their computer's processing power to solve complex mathematical problems that validate transactions and help to maintain the integrity of the blockchain network.

When a miner successfully validates a block of transactions, they are rewarded with a certain number of cryptocurrency tokens as a transaction fee and a newly created block reward. The amount of cryptocurrency rewarded varies depending on the network and can be adjusted over time.

To start mining, a miner needs to have specialized mining hardware and software, which are designed specifically for solving the mathematical problems required to validate transactions on the network. Miners also need to have access to cheap and reliable sources of electricity to power their mining hardware, as mining can be very energy-intensive.

Crypto mining can be a profitable activity, but it can also be expensive and requires a significant investment of time and resources. Additionally, as the difficulty of mining increases and the rewards decrease over time, it may become less profitable for individual miners to continue mining on their own.

Do not forget that not all cryptocurrencies can be mined, and the mining process can differ between cryptocurrencies. Some cryptocurrencies, such as Bitcoin, have a limited supply, which means that mining becomes progressively more difficult as more coins are mined, making it a competitive and challenging process. Other cryptocurrencies, such as Ethereum, are moving towards a different consensus mechanism that does not require mining.

Overall, crypto mining plays an important role in securing and maintaining the integrity of blockchain networks, and it's a fascinating and complex field that continues to evolve as new cryptocurrencies and mining techniques emerge.

How does mining work?

Cryptocurrency mining is like a game that uses your computer to help keep track of money transactions that people make using a digital currency. When you help verify these transactions, you earn some of the digital currency as a reward. Think of it like doing a job for the digital currency. The more you help out, the more you can earn.

To do this, you need a special computer that is designed to do this job. It's like having a gaming computer that's really good at playing one particular game. The computer has to do lots of complicated math problems to make sure the transactions are real and not fake.

Mining helps make sure that the digital currency is safe and can't be stolen or used for bad things. It's a bit like being a superhero for the digital currency world. However, mining uses a lot of energy, so it's important to be mindful of the impact it has on the environment.

Cryptocurrency mining is the process of adding new transactions to a blockchain network by solving complex mathematical algorithms using computational power. Miners use specialized hardware and software to participate in the network and compete to add new blocks to the blockchain, which contains a record of all transactions on the network.

The mining process involves verifying transactions, bundling them into blocks, and adding the blocks to the blockchain. When a miner solves the mathematical algorithm required to add a new block, they are rewarded with a certain amount of cryptocurrency, which serves as an incentive for them to continue participating in the network.

The algorithm that miners solve varies depending on the cryptocurrency they are mining. For example, Bitcoin uses a Proof-of-Work (PoW) algorithm, which requires miners to solve a complex math problem called a hash function. Ethereum, on the other hand, uses a Proof-of-Stake (PoS) algorithm, which rewards miners based on the amount of cryptocurrency they hold and stake to the network.

There are several types of cryptocurrency mining, including:

1. CPU Mining: This is the most basic form of mining, which uses a computer's Central Processing Unit (CPU) to perform the mining process. CPU mining is not very efficient and is generally only used for mining newer cryptocurrencies that do not have specialized hardware yet.

2. GPU Mining: This type of mining uses a computer's Graphics Processing Unit (GPU) to perform the mining process. GPUs are more efficient than CPUs and can

handle more complex algorithms, making them suitable for mining popular cryptocurrencies like Ethereum.

3. ASIC Mining: Application-Specific Integrated Circuit (ASIC) mining is the most advanced and efficient type of mining. ASICs are specialized hardware devices designed specifically for mining cryptocurrencies, and they are much faster and more energy-efficient than CPUs or GPUs. ASICs are typically used for mining popular cryptocurrencies like Bitcoin.

4. Cloud Mining: Cloud mining is a type of mining that involves renting mining hardware from a provider and paying a fee for their services. This is a popular option for those who do not have the resources or technical expertise to mine on their own.

CHAPTER FIVE

SECURITY

There are different types of wallets available and each one require different type of security measures. Some are hard and tangible and can be kept in safes and pockets and stores while others are cloud based and app based. The type of wallet will determine the type of security measure and tips to be taken.

Types of crypto wallets

There are several types of cryptocurrency wallets available, each with its own advantages and disadvantages. Here are the most common types of cryptocurrency wallets:

1. Hardware wallets: Hardware wallets are physical devices that store your cryptocurrencies offline and away from potential hackers. They are considered the most secure type of wallet and offer the highest level of

protection for your funds. Examples include Ledger and Trezor.

2. Software wallets: Software wallets are digital wallets that run on your computer or mobile device. They are more convenient to use than hardware wallets but are generally less secure. Examples include Exodus and Atomic Wallet.

3. Mobile wallets: Mobile wallets are software wallets that run on your mobile device. They are convenient to use and allow you to access your cryptocurrencies on the go. Examples include Mycelium and Trust Wallet.

4. Web wallets: Web wallets are wallets that run on a website or web-based platform. They are generally less secure than hardware or software wallets and are not recommended for storing large amounts of cryptocurrencies. Examples include Coinbase and Blockchain.info.

5. Paper wallets: Paper wallets are a physical piece of paper that contains your public and private keys for your cryptocurrencies. They are considered one of the safest ways to store cryptocurrencies as they are not connected to the internet. However, they can be easily lost or damaged if not stored properly.

The most common types of cryptocurrency wallets include hardware wallets, software wallets, mobile wallets, web wallets, and paper wallets. Each type of wallet has its own advantages and disadvantages, and it's important to choose the right wallet based on your needs and level of security required.

Tips for securing your cryptocurrency

Securing your cryptocurrency is crucial, as it is a digital asset that can be vulnerable to theft and hacking. Here are some tips for securing your cryptocurrency:

1. Use a reputable exchange: When buying and selling cryptocurrencies, use a reputable exchange that has a good reputation for security and reliability. Do your research and read reviews before choosing an exchange. Pay attention to con wallets. Example **cobra** wallet spelt as **cobbra** or **cobar**. Do not think of it as a typographical error, just stay clear. Also most legitimate wallets have a link to download their app from their website since play store to an extent is compromised, by that, I mean that caricature wallets can be uploaded as long as it has a different name.

2. Enable two-factor authentication (2FA): Enable 2FA on all of your cryptocurrency accounts. This will add an extra layer of security to your account by requiring a password and a unique code sent to your mobile device or email to log in.

3. Use a hardware wallet: A hardware wallet is a physical device that stores your cryptocurrencies offline and away from potential hackers. Consider using a hardware wallet such as Ledger or Trezor to store your cryptocurrencies.

4. Keep your private keys safe: Your private keys are like a password for your cryptocurrencies. Keep them safe and never share them with anyone. Consider storing them in a secure location such as a safety deposit box.

5. Use strong passwords: Use strong, unique passwords for all of your cryptocurrency accounts and change them regularly. Avoid using easily guessable passwords such as your name or birthdate.

6. Use a VPN: Use a virtual private network (VPN) to encrypt your internet connection and protect your online activities from potential hackers. It will also be wise not to use any random VPN because they are free or cheap. Hackers can create such type to steal your login information. So be sure to activate 2F authentication, that way it will take more than username and password to access your account, providing extra security.

7. Stay informed: Stay up to date with the latest security risks and trends in the cryptocurrency industry. Follow reputable news sources and security experts on social media to stay informed. Keeping your cryptocurrencies

safe is very important, as they are digital assets that can be vulnerable to hacking and theft.

In conclusion, keeping your cryptocurrencies safe requires using reputable exchanges, enabling two-factor authentication, using a hardware wallet, using strong passwords, keeping your private keys safe, and staying informed about the latest security risks. By following these tips, you can help protect your cryptocurrencies from potential threats and keep them safe.

CHAPTER SIX

EXCHANGES

What are crypto exchanges?

Crypto exchanges are platforms that allow users to buy, sell, and trade cryptocurrencies. These exchanges act as intermediaries between buyers and sellers, providing a platform for users to exchange their cryptocurrencies for other digital assets or fiat currencies.

There are several types of crypto exchanges

1. Centralized exchanges (CEX): These are the most common type of exchange, where transactions are facilitated by a centralized authority. They are popular due to their user-friendly interface and high liquidity. Examples include Binance, Coinbase, and Kraken.

2. Decentralized exchanges (DEX): These exchanges use smart contracts on a blockchain to facilitate transactions, removing the need for a centralized

authority. They are less user-friendly but offer more privacy and security. Examples include Uniswap and PancakeSwap.

3. Peer-to-peer (P2P) exchanges: These exchanges allow users to buy and sell cryptocurrencies directly with other individuals, without the need for a centralized authority. Examples include LocalBitcoins and Paxful.

Before choosing a wallet or exchange

When choosing an exchange, consider factors such as security, liquidity, fees, reputation, and user interface.

1. Security: Security should be your top priority when choosing a crypto exchange. Look for an exchange that has a strong track record for security and takes measures to protect user funds, such as two-factor authentication (2FA), cold storage of funds, and insurance against theft or hacking. You should also consider the exchange's history of security breaches and how it responded to those incidents.

2. Liquidity: Liquidity refers to the ability to buy and sell cryptocurrencies quickly and at a fair price. Choose an exchange with high liquidity to ensure that you can quickly buy and sell your cryptocurrencies at a fair price. You can check an exchange's liquidity by looking at its trading volume and order book.

3. Fees: Consider the fees charged by the exchange for transactions, withdrawals, and deposits. Look for an exchange with low fees to minimize costs. Some exchanges charge a flat fee per transaction, while others charge a percentage of the transaction amount. You should also consider the exchange's deposit and withdrawal fees, which can vary depending on the payment method you use.

4. Reputation: Choose an exchange with a good reputation and positive reviews from other users. You can research an exchange's reputation by reading online reviews, checking its social media presence, and looking at its history of regulatory compliance. You should also consider the exchange's customer support, as prompt and helpful customer support can make a big difference if you encounter any issues.

5. User interface: Choose an exchange with a user-friendly interface that makes it easy to buy, sell, and trade cryptocurrencies. Look for an exchange with a clear and intuitive user interface, a wide range of trading pairs, and helpful features such as price charts and order history. You should also consider the exchange's mobile app if you plan to trade on the go.

Finally, when choosing a crypto exchange, you should prioritize security, liquidity, low fees, a good reputation, and a user-friendly interface. By considering these factors, you can find an exchange that meets your needs and helps you buy, sell, and trade cryptocurrencies with confidence.

The above is listed in the scale of importance. Security is number one, then liquidity, after that, fees before reviews and looks. Reviews are personal opinion and may align differently to what you want.

CHAPTER SEVEN

TRADING

Trading is the act of buying and selling assets in order to make a profit. In the case of cryptocurrencies, trading involves buying and selling digital assets such as Bitcoin, Ethereum, or other altcoins.

Types of trading

There are several types of trading in the cryptocurrency market. The few listed here are the most popular

1. Day trading: Day trading involves buying and selling cryptocurrencies within the same day to take advantage of short-term price movements. This practice is suited for large investors, those who 0.5 to 2 percent change can make a substantial difference in their profit. For beginners, you can only use this strategy to practice by using small amount of money until you feel confident to trade with lump sum.

2. Swing trading: Swing trading involves holding cryptocurrencies for a few days or weeks to take advantage of medium-term price movements. I use this a lot since I am not a large investor, I will need about 5 to 10 percent change in the price either as bull or bear for me to make a worthwhile profit. You will need to make research to find out things that affects the coins you want to focus on.

3. Position trading: Position trading involves holding cryptocurrencies for an extended period of time, usually several months or years, to take advantage of long-term price movements.

4. Scalping: Scalping involves making quick trades to take advantage of small price movements, often within seconds or minutes. Unlike day trading, Scalping can be done several times within 24 hours.

5. Algorithmic trading: Algorithmic trading involves using software or bots to execute trades automatically based on predefined rules. This is already becoming popular as artificial intelligence becomes more prevalent. Algorithm trading can take the form of any trading above. And there is almost no chance of losing a buy or sell opportunity. While this has record a lot of success, a little mistake in terms of configuration can run your capital to the ground.

Here are some tips for successful cryptocurrency trading:

1. Develop a trading plan: This is an essential step before you start trading. Your trading plan should outline your goals, risk tolerance, and trading strategy. Having a plan in place will help you stay focused and avoid emotional decision-making. Your plan should also include guidelines for managing your risk, such as stop-loss orders and position sizing.

2. Learn technical analysis: Technical analysis is the process of using price charts and other indicators to analyze price movements and identify trends. By learning how to read price charts and use technical analysis tools, you can make more informed trading decisions. Technical analysis can help you identify support and resistance levels, trend lines, and chart patterns that can indicate whether a cryptocurrency's price is likely to go up or down.

3. Keep up with news and market trends: Cryptocurrency markets can be highly volatile, and prices can be influenced by a range of factors such as news events, regulatory changes, and market sentiment. Keeping up with the latest news and market trends can help you stay ahead of the curve and make informed trading decisions. For example, if a major news event affects

the value of a particular cryptocurrency, you can adjust your trading strategy accordingly

4. Manage your risk: Trading cryptocurrencies can be risky, so it's important to manage your risk carefully. This includes setting stop-loss orders to limit your losses, diversifying your portfolio, and avoiding overtrading. Setting stop-loss orders can help you limit your potential losses if a cryptocurrency's price suddenly drops. Diversifying your portfolio can help you spread your risk across multiple assets, reducing your exposure to any single cryptocurrency. Overtrading, or making too many trades too quickly, can increase your risk of making poor trading decisions based on emotion rather than logic.

5. Choose a reliable exchange: When trading cryptocurrencies, it's important to choose a reliable exchange that offers security, liquidity, and low fees. Do your research and choose an exchange with a good reputation and positive reviews from other users. You should also consider the exchange's security measures, such as two-factor authentication and cold storage for user funds. High liquidity can help ensure that you can buy and sell cryptocurrencies quickly and easily, while low fees can help maximize your profits.

6. Start small and gradually increase your position: It's important to start small when you're first getting

started with cryptocurrency trading. This will help you get a feel for the market and avoid making big mistakes early on. Once you're more comfortable with the market, you can gradually increase the size of your trades.

7. Have patience and discipline: Successful cryptocurrency trading requires patience and discipline. It's important to stick to your trading plan and avoid making emotional decisions based on fear or greed. This can be challenging, especially when the market is volatile, but it's essential for long-term success.

8. Use dollar-cost averaging: Dollar-cost averaging is a strategy where you invest a fixed amount of money at regular intervals, regardless of the cryptocurrency's price. This can help you avoid buying at the top of the market and selling at the bottom. Over time, this can help you accumulate more cryptocurrency at a lower average cost.

9. Keep track of your trades and performance: It's important to keep track of your trades and performance over time. This can help you identify what's working and what's not, and make adjustments to your trading plan accordingly. You can use a spreadsheet or trading journal to keep track of your trades, including the

cryptocurrency, the price, the date, and the size of the trade.

10. Be prepared for market volatility: Cryptocurrency markets can be highly volatile, and prices can fluctuate rapidly. It's important to be prepared for this and avoid making impulsive decisions based on short-term price movements. Instead, focus on the long-term trends and stick to your trading plan. It's also a good idea to have a plan in place for managing risk during periods of high volatility. This might include setting tighter stop-loss orders or reducing your position size.

Chapter Eight

Investing

Cryptocurrencies have become increasingly popular over the past few years, with more and more people investing in them. However, investing in cryptocurrencies is not without its risks. In this article, we will explore how to invest in cryptocurrencies, the risks and rewards of investing in them, and strategies for investing in cryptocurrencies.

How to Invest in Cryptocurrencies:

a. Do Your Research: Before investing in cryptocurrencies, it is essential to do your research. You need to understand how cryptocurrencies work, their underlying technology, the market trends, and the potential risks and rewards of investing in them. You can do this by reading articles, watching videos, and attending cryptocurrency seminars.

b. Choose a Cryptocurrency Exchange: This cannot be overemphasized. A cryptocurrency exchange is an online platform that allows you to buy, sell, and trade cryptocurrencies. There are numerous cryptocurrency exchanges, and it is important to choose one that is secure, reliable, and has a good reputation. Some of the popular cryptocurrency exchanges include Coinbase, Binance, Kraken, and Bitfinex.

c. Create a Wallet: A cryptocurrency wallet is a digital wallet that allows you to store, send, and receive cryptocurrencies. There are various types of cryptocurrency wallets, including hardware wallets, software wallets, and online wallets. It is important to choose a wallet that is secure and easy to use.

d. Choose the Cryptocurrencies to invest in: There are numerous cryptocurrencies available, and it is important to choose the ones that you believe have the most potential. Some of the popular cryptocurrencies include Bitcoin, Ethereum, Litecoin, Ripple, and Bitcoin Cash. You can use market analysis and technical analysis to determine which cryptocurrencies are likely to perform well.

e. Invest and Monitor: Once you have chosen the cryptocurrencies to invest in, you can buy them using your chosen cryptocurrency exchange. It is important to monitor the market trends and your investments regularly to determine when to sell or hold your cryptocurrencies

Risks and rewards of investing in cryptocurrencies

Investing in cryptocurrencies comes with both risks and rewards. Here are some of the risks and rewards of investing in cryptocurrencies:

Risks

i. Volatility: Cryptocurrencies are highly volatile, and their prices can fluctuate significantly within a short period. This means that you can make a lot of money in a short time, but you can also lose a lot of money.

ii. Regulatory Risks: Cryptocurrencies are not yet regulated in many countries, which means that they are not protected by government regulations. This can make them vulnerable to fraud, hacking, and other criminal activities.

iii. Market Risks: Cryptocurrencies are influenced by market trends, and their prices can be affected by various factors such as news, government policies, and economic events.

iv. Cybersecurity Risks: Cryptocurrencies are stored in digital wallets, which can be vulnerable to cyber-attacks, hacking, and other forms of cybercrime.

v. Liquidity Risks: Cryptocurrencies are not as liquid as traditional investments such as stocks, bonds, and mutual funds. This means that it may be difficult to sell your cryptocurrencies quickly, especially during times of market instability.

vi. Adoption Risks: The adoption of cryptocurrencies is still limited, and not all businesses and individuals accept cryptocurrencies as a form of payment. This means that the demand for cryptocurrencies may not be as high as expected, which can lead to a decline in their value. Additionally, if governments or financial institutions do not adopt or recognize cryptocurrencies, it could impact their long-term viability.

Rewards

i. High Returns: Cryptocurrencies have the potential to generate high returns, and some investors have made a lot of money by investing in them.

ii. Diversification: Investing in cryptocurrencies can provide diversification to your investment portfolio, which can reduce the overall risk.

iii. Accessibility: Cryptocurrencies are accessible to anyone with an internet connection, which means that you can invest in them from anywhere in the world.

iv. Decentralization: Cryptocurrencies are decentralized, which means that they are not controlled by any government or financial institution. This provides a level of privacy and security that is not available with traditional financial systems.

v. Potential for High Returns: Cryptocurrencies have the potential to generate high returns for investors. In the past, some cryptocurrencies have increased in value by several thousand percent. Although the returns are not guaranteed, the potential for high returns is one of the main reasons why many investors are attracted to cryptocurrencies.

vi. Lower Transaction Costs: Transaction costs for cryptocurrencies are often lower than those for traditional investments such as stocks, bonds, and mutual funds. This is because cryptocurrencies do not require intermediaries such as brokers or custodians, which can reduce transaction costs for investors. Additionally, because cryptocurrencies are digital assets, they can be transferred and exchanged quickly and easily, which can further reduce transaction costs.

Strategies for investing in cryptocurrencies

Some strategies for investing in cryptocurrencies

1. Dollar-Cost Averaging: Dollar-cost averaging is a strategy that involves investing a fixed amount of money at regular intervals. This strategy can help reduce the impact of market volatility on the strategy of dollar-cost averaging: For example, instead of investing a lump sum of $10,000 in Bitcoin at one time, you can invest $1,000 every month for ten months. This strategy can help you avoid investing at the wrong time when the market is at its peak, and you can take advantage of buying when the price is low.

2. Long-Term Investment: Cryptocurrencies are highly volatile, and their prices can fluctuate significantly in the short term. However, over the long term, the market tends to move in an upward direction. Therefore, it is important to adopt a long-term investment strategy when investing in cryptocurrencies.

3. Diversification: Diversification is a strategy that involves investing in a variety of assets to reduce the overall risk. This strategy can also be applied to cryptocurrencies by investing in different types of cryptocurrencies, such as Bitcoin, Ethereum, Litecoin, and Ripple.

4. Research and Analysis: Before investing in cryptocurrencies, it is important to conduct thorough research and analysis. You should look at market trends, technical analysis, and fundamental analysis to determine which cryptocurrencies are likely to perform well.

5. Set a Stop Loss: A stop-loss is an order to sell a cryptocurrency when the price reaches a certain level. This can help you minimize your losses in case the market takes a sudden downturn. Stay Updated: Cryptocurrencies are highly volatile, and their prices can be affected by various factors such as news, government policies, and economic events. Therefore, it is important to stay updated with the latest news and events that may affect the cryptocurrency market.

Conclusion

Investing in cryptocurrencies can be highly rewarding, but it also comes with significant risks. It is therefore wise to do your research, choose a reliable cryptocurrency exchange and wallet, and adopt a long-term investment strategy. You should also diversify your portfolio and stay updated with the latest market trends and events. With these strategies, you can maximize your rewards and minimize your risks when investing in cryptocurrencies.

Chapter Nine

ICOs and STOs

ICOs and STOs are fundraising methods that allow companies to raise capital by issuing and selling tokens to investors. In this section, we will discuss what ICOs and STOs are, how they work, and the risks and rewards of investing in them.

What are ICOs?

ICOs, or Initial Coin Offerings, are a type of fundraising method in which companies issue and sell digital tokens to investors. These tokens are typically created on a blockchain platform and are designed to have some type of utility or function within the company's ecosystem. ICO investors are typically offered these tokens in exchange for other cryptocurrencies such as Bitcoin or Ethereum. These tokens can then be traded on cryptocurrency exchanges, where their value is determined by supply and demand.

What are STOs?

STOs, or Security Token Offerings, are a type of fundraising method in which companies issue and sell digital tokens that represent ownership in a company or asset. STOs are often used to raise capital for real estate or private equity investments.

STO investors are typically offered these tokens in exchange for fiat currency or other cryptocurrencies. These tokens are typically regulated by securities laws and are subject to disclosure and reporting requirements.

How do ICOs and STOs work?

ICOs and STOs both work by allowing companies to raise capital by issuing and selling digital tokens to investors. However, the key difference between ICOs and STOs is the nature of the tokens being sold.

ICOs typically involve the issuance and sale of utility tokens, which are designed to have some type of utility or function within the company's ecosystem. Investors who purchase utility tokens are typically interested in using the tokens within the company's ecosystem, or speculating on their future value.

STOs, on the other hand, involve the issuance and sale of security tokens, which are designed to represent ownership in a company or asset. Investors who purchase security tokens are typically interested in receiving a return on their investment, either through dividends or the appreciation of the token's value.

Risks and Rewards of Investing in ICOs and STOs

Investing in ICOs and STOs can be highly rewarding, but it also comes with significant risks. Listed below are some of the risks and rewards of investing in ICOs and STOs:

Risks of Investing in ICOs and STOs

i.   Lack of Regulation: ICOs and STOs are still largely unregulated, which means that investors are not protected by the same level of regulation as traditional investments such as stocks and bonds. This can make ICOs and STOs more susceptible to fraud and other forms of manipulation.

ii. High Volatility: The value of ICO and STO tokens can be highly volatile, which means that their value can fluctuate significantly in a short period of time. This volatility can be caused by a variety of factors, including changes in market sentiment and fluctuations in the value of other cryptocurrencies.

iii. Liquidity Risks: ICOs and STOs may be illiquid, which means that it may be difficult to sell your tokens quickly, especially during times of market instability. Additionally, many ICO and STO tokens are not listed on major cryptocurrency exchanges, which can further reduce their liquidity.

iv. Lack of Investor Protections: ICOs and STOs may not offer the same level of investor protections as traditional investments. Because these offerings are often unregulated, investors may not have the same rights or protections as they would with a traditional investment. For example, they may not have access to information about the company or project, and they may not be able to exercise their rights as investors in the event of a dispute.

Rewards of Investing in ICOs and STOs

i. Potential for High Returns: ICOs and STOs have the potential to generate high returns for i0nvestors, especially in the early stages of the project. In the past, some ICOs and STOs have generated returns of several thousand percent.

ii. Access to New Markets: ICOs and STOs can provide investors with access to new markets and investment opportunities that may not be available through traditional investments.

iii. Decentralization: ICOs and STOs are often associated with decentralization, which means that they are not controlled by any central authority or institution. This can be seen as a positive aspect.

iv. Democratization of investment Opportunities: ICOs and STOs have the potential to democratize investment opportunities, by providing access to investment opportunities that were previously only available to institutional investors or high-net-worth individuals. This can help to level the playing field and provide more opportunities for retail investors to invest in innovative projects.

v.   Flexibility ICOs and STOs offer greater flexibility compared to traditional investments, such as stocks or bonds. Investors can choose to invest in a variety of projects, with varying levels of risk and return. Additionally, ICO and STO tokens can be traded on cryptocurrency exchanges, which provides investors with greater flexibility to buy, sell or trade their holdings.

It is worthy to note that investing in ICOs and STOs can be risky, and investors should do their due diligence and thoroughly research any project or company before investing. Additionally, investors should only invest money that they can afford to lose, as there is no guarantee of returns.

CHAPTER TEN

REGULATIONS

Regulations on cryptocurrencies vary greatly from country to country and even from state to state within the same country. Some countries have embraced cryptocurrencies and have implemented favorable regulations, while others have banned them outright. Here, we will discuss the current state of regulations on cryptocurrencies, how they affect the cryptocurrency market, and what the future of cryptocurrency regulations may hold.

Current Regulations on Cryptocurrencies

The regulatory landscape for cryptocurrencies is still in its early stages, with many countries yet to adopt a clear stance. However, there are some countries that have implemented specific regulations for cryptocurrencies, while others are still considering how best to regulate them.

In the United States, cryptocurrencies are classified as property for tax purposes, which means that they are subject to capital gains taxes. The IRS has also issued guidelines on how cryptocurrencies should be reported on tax returns. Additionally, some states have implemented their own regulations, such as New York's BitLicense, which requires companies to obtain a license to operate in the state.

In Japan, cryptocurrencies are recognized as a legal form of payment, and exchanges are required to register with the Financial Services Agency (FSA) and comply with certain regulations. South Korea has also implemented regulations for cryptocurrencies, requiring exchanges to comply with anti-money laundering (AML) and know-your-customer (KYC) regulations.

In contrast, China has banned all cryptocurrency-related activities, including trading, mining, and initial coin offerings (ICOs). India has also taken a hardline stance on cryptocurrencies, with the government indicating that it plans to ban them altogether.

How Regulations Affect the Cryptocurrency Market

Regulations can have a significant impact on the cryptocurrency market. Favorable regulations can help to legitimize cryptocurrencies and increase adoption, while unfavorable regulations can stifle innovation and limit growth.

For example, Japan's favorable regulatory environment has led to a surge in cryptocurrency adoption, with many businesses now accepting cryptocurrencies as payment. In contrast, China's ban on cryptocurrencies has had a significant impact on the market, with many Chinese investors being forced to sell their holdings and move their funds offshore.

In the United States, the regulatory environment has had a mixed impact on the market. While the recognition of cryptocurrencies as property has provided some clarity for investors and businesses, the lack of clear regulations for ICOs has led to uncertainty and confusion.

Future of Cryptocurrency Regulations

The future of cryptocurrency regulations is still unclear, but there are several trends that are emerging. Many countries are beginning to recognize the potential of cryptocurrencies and blockchain technology and are working to implement favorable regulations. This includes countries such as Singapore, Switzerland, and Malta, which have implemented regulations designed to attract blockchain and cryptocurrency businesses.

At the same time, there are still many countries that are grappling with how best to regulate cryptocurrencies. Some are considering implementing regulations similar to those in Japan, while others are looking to more heavily restrict or even ban cryptocurrencies altogether.

In the United States, there is a growing push for clearer regulations on cryptocurrencies and ICOs. Several bills have been introduced in Congress that would provide more clarity and certainty for investors and businesses.

Overall, the future of cryptocurrency regulations is likely to be shaped by a combination of factors, including technological innovation, geopolitical tensions, and economic factors. As the cryptocurrency market continues to evolve and mature, it is likely that we will see more countries adopting regulations and developing their own approaches to managing cryptocurrencies.

CHAPTER ELEVEN

REAL-WORLD APPLICATIONS OF CRYPTOCURRENCY

Cryptocurrencies have been gaining increasing popularity over the past few years, and many industries are starting to incorporate them into their operations. Here, we will discuss how cryptocurrencies are being used in the real world, provide examples of industries using cryptocurrencies, and explore the potential for cryptocurrencies in the future.

How Cryptocurrencies are Being Used in the Real World

Cryptocurrencies are being used in a variety of ways in the real world, from everyday purchases to cross-border payments. One of the main advantages of cryptocurrencies is that they can be used to make transactions without the need for a central authority, such as a bank or government.

Some of the most common ways that cryptocurrencies are being used in the real world include:

a. Online purchases: Many online retailers now accept cryptocurrencies as a form of payment. This includes major companies such as Microsoft, Overstock.com, and Shopify.

b. Cross-border payments: Cryptocurrencies can be used to make cross-border payments quickly and inexpensively, without the need for intermediaries such as banks.

c. Remittances: Cryptocurrencies can also be used to send remittances to family members or friends in other countries, again without the need for intermediaries.

d. Investment: Many people are investing in cryptocurrencies as a way to diversify their portfolios and potentially earn high returns.

Examples of Industries Using Cryptocurrency

Cryptocurrencies are being used in a variety of industries, from finance to healthcare to entertainment. Here are some examples:

1. Finance: Many financial institutions are experimenting with cryptocurrencies, including JPMorgan Chase, Goldman Sachs, and Fidelity. Some are exploring the

use of cryptocurrencies for cross-border payments, while others are investing in cryptocurrencies as an asset class.

2. Healthcare: Cryptocurrencies are being used in the healthcare industry to store and share patient data securely. This includes companies such as Patientory and SimplyVital Health.

3. Gaming and Entertainment: Cryptocurrencies are also being used in the gaming and entertainment industries, such as for in-game purchases and ticket sales. Companies such as Enjin and Guts Gaming are leading the way in this area.

4. Real Estate: Cryptocurrencies are being used in real estate transactions, with some companies accepting cryptocurrencies as a form of payment for properties.

5. Travel: Cryptocurrencies are being used in the travel industry for booking flights, hotels, and other travel-related expenses. For example, CheapAir.com is one travel company that accepts Bitcoin as a form of payment. Charity: Cryptocurrencies are being used in the charitable sector, with some organizations accepting donations in the form of cryptocurrencies. This includes organizations such as The Water Project, which accepts Bitcoin donations to provide clean water to communities in need.

Potential for Cryptocurrency in the Future

The potential for cryptocurrencies in the future is vast and varied. While cryptocurrencies are still in their early stages, they have the potential to revolutionize the way that we make transactions and store value. Here are some potential use cases for cryptocurrencies in the future:

i. Decentralized Finance (DeFi): DeFi is a rapidly growing area that uses cryptocurrencies to provide financial services without the need for traditional financial institutions. This includes services such as lending, borrowing, and trading.

ii. Digital Identity: Cryptocurrencies can be used to create secure digital identities, allowing people to store and share their personal data in a secure and private way.

iii. Supply Chain Management: Cryptocurrencies can be used to track products as they move through the supply chain, providing greater transparency and reducing the risk of fraud.

iv. Micropayments: Cryptocurrencies can be used for micropayments, which are small transactions that are not feasible using traditional payment methods. This could be particularly useful for content creators, who could receive small payments for their work.

Overall, the potential for cryptocurrencies in the future is vast and varied. While there are still many challenges to overcome, such as scalability and regulation, the potential benefits of cryptocurrencies are significant. As the technology continues to evolve and mature, it is likely that we will see more industries incorporating cryptocurrencies into their operations, and new use cases emerging.

CHAPTER TWELVE

COMMON MISTAKES TO AVOID

As with any new venture, there is a learning curve when it comes to investing in cryptocurrency. Unfortunately, many beginners make mistakes that can cost them money or even lead to loss of funds. Here are some common mistakes that beginners make when getting started with cryptocurrency:

i. Failing to do their own research: Many beginners jump into investing in cryptocurrency without doing their own research. They rely on tips from friends or social media influencers and invest in cryptocurrencies without fully understanding what they are investing in. This can lead to poor investment decisions and significant losses.

ii. Investing more than they can afford to lose: Cryptocurrency is a high-risk investment, and beginners should only invest money that they can afford to lose. Many beginners invest more than they should, hoping for a quick return on their investment. This can lead to financial stress and potentially devastating losses.

iii. Not securing their cryptocurrency: Cryptocurrencies are stored in digital wallets, and it is essential to keep these wallets secure. Many beginners fail to take the necessary precautions to secure their wallets, leaving themselves vulnerable to hacks and theft. Theft has led to more loss in crypto assets than wrong trading, so keeping your seeds and phrases safe as well as not linking your credit or debit cards to a trading platform as beginners is vital. Refer to chapter five for more details.

iv. Failing to diversify their portfolio: Many beginners invest all of their money in a single cryptocurrency, hoping that it will increase in value. However, this is a risky strategy, and diversifying their portfolio can help reduce risk and potentially increase returns.

v. Not understanding market volatility: Cryptocurrency markets are highly volatile, and beginners need to understand that the value of their investment can fluctuate significantly in a short period. They should be prepared for this volatility and not panic when the market dips.

vi. Not keeping track of taxes: Many beginners do not realize that they are required to report their cryptocurrency gains and losses on their taxes. Failure to do so can result in penalties and fines.

vii. Falling for scams: Unfortunately, the cryptocurrency market is rife with scams, and many beginners fall victim to them. Scams can come in the form of fake ICOs, phishing emails, or Ponzi schemes. Beginners should be wary of any investment opportunity that seems too good to be true.

viii. Trading too frequently: Cryptocurrency trading can be addictive, and some beginners may be tempted to trade frequently to try to earn quick profits. However, this is a risky strategy that can lead to significant losses.

ix. Not taking profits: Many beginners hold onto their cryptocurrency investment for too long, hoping for further gains. However, it is essential to take profits along the way to lock in gains and reduce risk.

Overall, investing in cryptocurrency can be a profitable venture, but beginners need to be careful and avoid these common mistakes. To avoid these common mistakes, beginners should take the time to research and learn about cryptocurrencies before investing any money. They should also use reputable cryptocurrency exchanges and wallets and avoid falling for scams or hype-driven investments. By taking a cautious and informed approach, beginners can increase their chances of success in the cryptocurrency market.

GLOSSARY

Here are fifty words related to cryptocurrency and a brief explanation.

1. Bitcoin: The first and most well-known cryptocurrency, created in 2009.
2. Blockchain: A decentralized, digital ledger that records transactions in a secure and transparent manner.
3. Altcoin: Any cryptocurrency that is not Bitcoin.
4. Mining: The process of verifying transactions and adding them to the blockchain, typically through the use of powerful computers.
5. Wallet: A digital wallet used to store and manage cryptocurrency.
6. Fork: A change in the code of a cryptocurrency that creates a new, separate version of the blockchain.
7. Exchange: A platform that allows users to buy, sell, and trade cryptocurrencies.
8. ICO: Initial Coin Offering, a fundraising mechanism used by cryptocurrency startups to raise capital by selling new tokens to investors.
9. ICO Scam: A fraudulent ICO in which the founders abscond with investors' money.

10. Smart Contract: A self-executing contract that is coded on the blockchain and automatically executes when certain conditions are met.

11. Token: A unit of value created and used by a particular blockchain.

12. Hash Rate: The speed at which a computer can process transactions and add them to the blockchain.

13. Hard Fork: A type of fork in which the new blockchain is not backwards compatible with the old blockchain.

14. Soft Fork: A type of fork in which the new blockchain is backwards compatible with the old blockchain.

15. Cryptography: The practice of secure communication in the presence of third parties.

16. Public Key: A code used to receive cryptocurrency.

17. Private Key: A code used to send cryptocurrency.

18. Proof of Work: A consensus algorithm used to verify transactions on the blockchain.

19. Proof of Stake: A consensus algorithm that requires users to stake their cryptocurrency in order to verify transactions.

20. Decentralized: A system in which there is no central authority controlling the network.

21. Centralized: A system in which there is a central authority controlling the network.

22. Whitepaper: A detailed document that outlines the technology, team, and goals of a cryptocurrency project.

23. Market Cap: The total value of all coins in circulation.

24. HODL: A misspelling of "hold," used in the cryptocurrency community to encourage investors to hold onto their coins despite market fluctuations.

25. FOMO: Fear of Missing Out, a feeling of anxiety that one may miss an opportunity to profit from cryptocurrency investments.

26. FUD: Fear, Uncertainty, and Doubt, a tactic used to spread negative information and decrease investor confidence in a particular cryptocurrency.

27. Whale: A term used to describe investors with large amounts of cryptocurrency holdings.

28. Satoshi: The smallest unit of measurement in Bitcoin, equal to 0.00000001 BTC.

29. Gas: The fee required to execute a smart contract on the Ethereum network.

30. Cold Storage: The practice of storing cryptocurrency offline in order to protect it from hacks or other security breaches.

31. DApp: Decentralized application, an application that runs on a decentralized blockchain network.

32. DAO: Decentralized Autonomous Organization, an organization that operates through smart contracts and is controlled by its members.

33. ERC-20: A standard for creating tokens on the Ethereum blockchain.

34. ICO Airdrop: A method of distributing free tokens to the community in order to generate interest in an upcoming ICO.

35. KYC: Know Your Customer, a process used to verify the identity of customers to prevent fraud and money laundering.

36. Lightning Network: A protocol for instant Bitcoin transactions that aims to reduce transaction fees and increase scalability.

37. Non-fungible Token (NFT): A unique token that represents a specific asset, such as digital art or collectibles.

38. Nodes: Computers or servers that participate in validating transactions on a blockchain network.

39. Proof of Concept (POC): A demonstration that a particular technology or idea is viable.

40. Satoshi Nakamoto: The pseudonym used by the unknown creator(s) of Bitcoin.

41. SegWit: Segregated Witness, a protocol upgrade that increases the block size limit on the Bitcoin blockchain.

42. Smart Property: Physical assets that are controlled and tracked using smart contracts on a blockchain.

43. Soft Cap: The minimum amount of funds required for an ICO to be considered successful.

44. Stablecoin: A cryptocurrency that is designed to maintain a stable value, often pegged to a fiat currency or commodity.

45. Token Sale: A process for selling tokens to investors during an ICO.

46. White Hat Hacker: A hacker who uses their skills for ethical purposes, such as identifying vulnerabilities in a blockchain network.

47. Yellow Paper: A document that outlines the technical details of a particular blockchain project.

48. 2FA: Two-Factor Authentication, a security feature that requires users to provide two forms of authentication in order to access an account.

49. Atomic Swap: A peer-to-peer exchange of cryptocurrencies without the need for a centralized exchange.

50. Block Reward: The amount of cryptocurrency awarded to miners for successfully mining a new block on the blockchain.

AFTERWORD

Some Exchangers, wallets and platforms were mentioned in the course of this book and are not in any way a validation by the author. It is expected that anyone who has a knack for cryptocurrency investment should be ready to do their own research. My next book Crypto 102 will give insight on some method of research and practical guide to trading. Be sure to look it up when it is released.